This big kid book
belongs to:

PADDY PIGS' WEANING ADVENTURE

Paddy Pig is
growing up;
he's getting big
and

STRONG!

and as he grows,
mom's milk will go.

Bring on his next
adventure!

It's time to wean for Paddy Pig, What else could make him smile?

A pile of mud!
Squishy and smooth,
he'll never want to
move.

and when night falls, curl in and cuddle...

Mommy Pig will
always snuggle!

It's time to wean
for
Paddy Pig

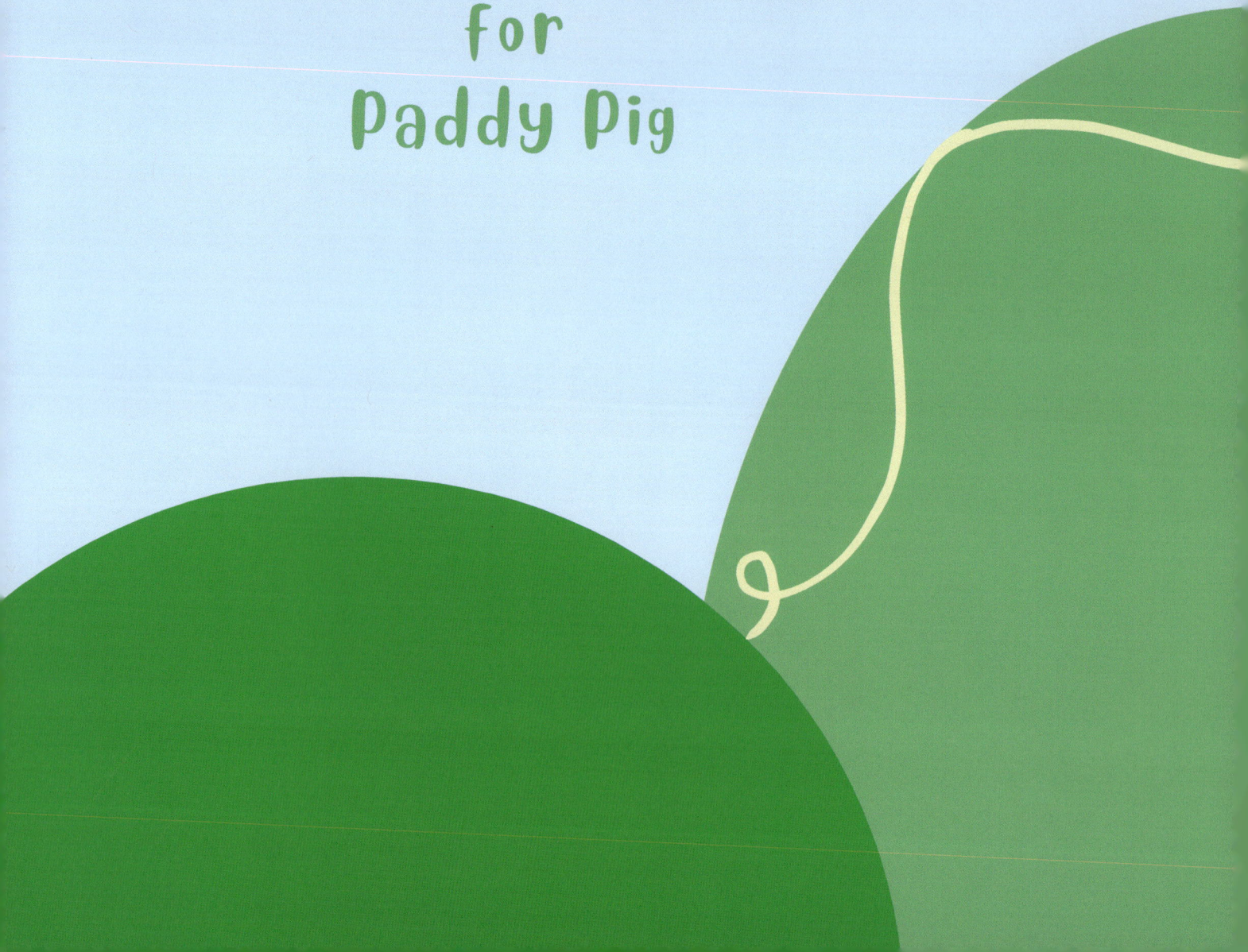

What else could
make him squeal?

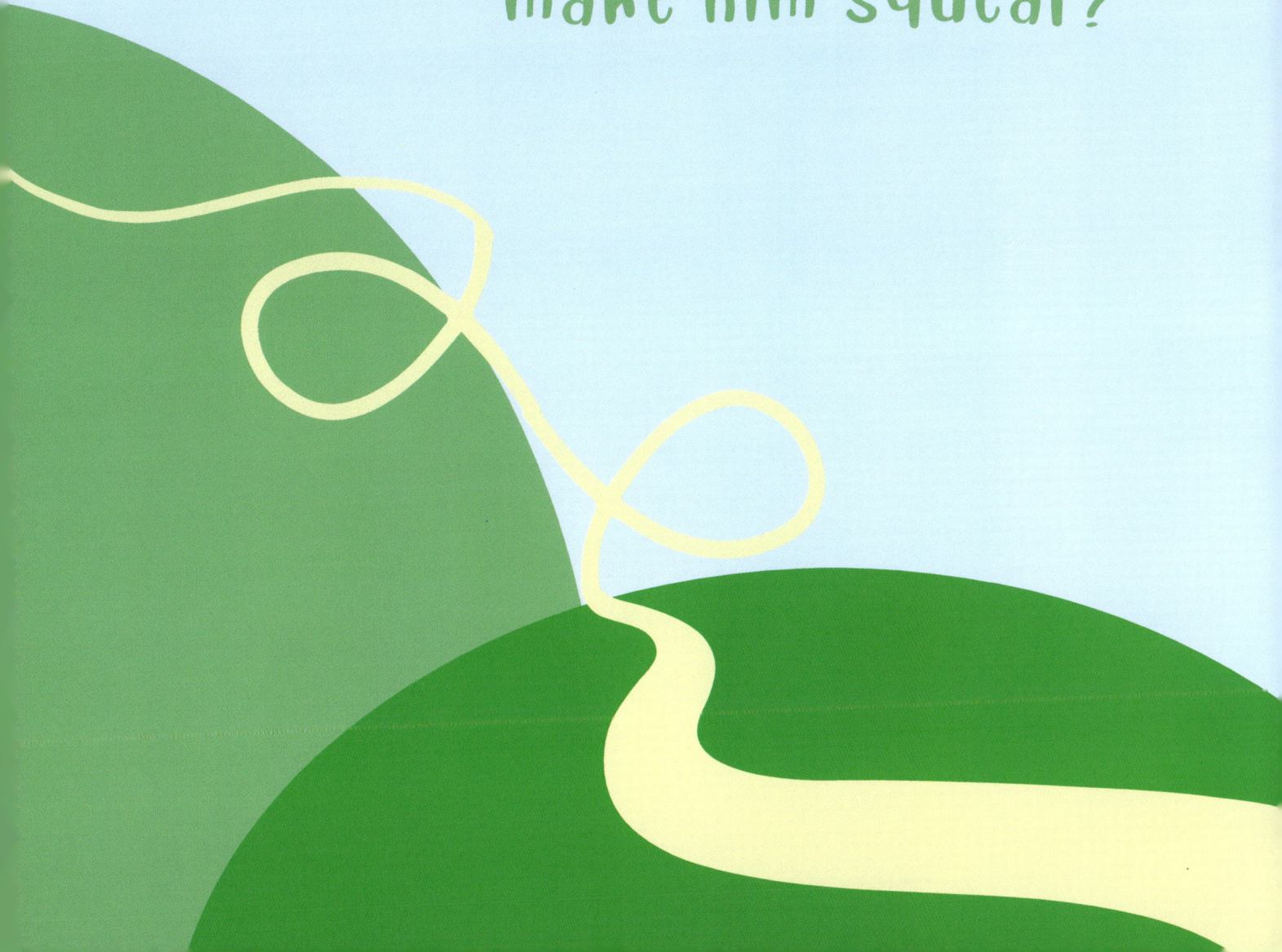

A great adventure in the wind, fly and glide and spin

and when night
falls,
curl in and cuddle...

Mommy Pig
will always
snuggle!

It's time to wean for Paddy Pig. What else could fill his belly?

Choc mud milk shakes and curly fries! What else lies in his sty?

and when night falls
curl in and cuddle,...

Mommy Pig
will always
snuggle!

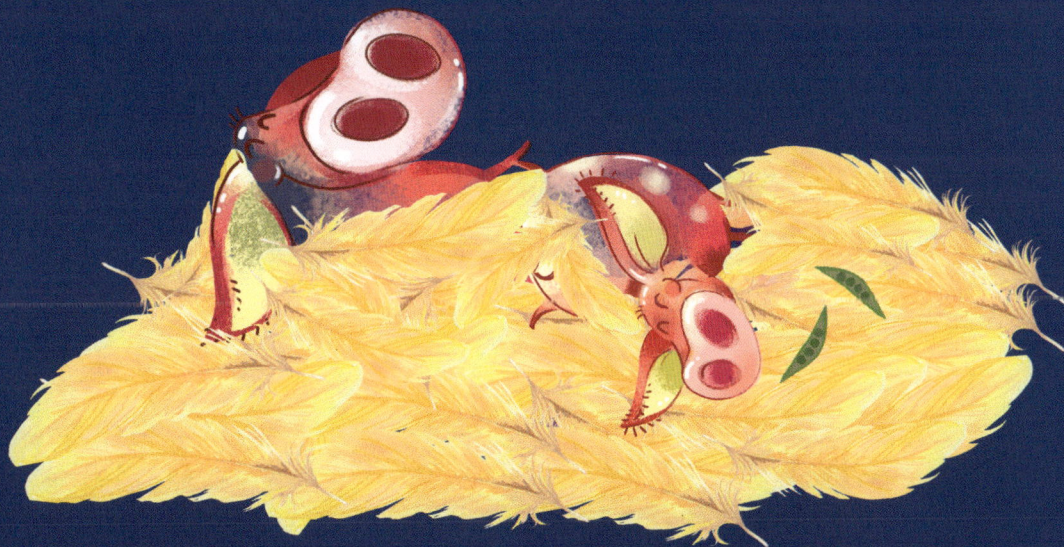

It's time to wean for Paddy Pig. What else could help him relax?

A big, deep breath, have some space... embrace your favourite place

and when night falls
curl in and cuddle...

Mommy Pig
will always
snuggle!

It's time to wean
for Paddy Pig.
What else could
help him sleep?

A cuddly bear, no need
to fear! Soft friends
can be so neat

and when night falls
curl in and cuddle…

Mommy pig
will always
snuggle!

It's time to wean for you, my darling.

What fun adventures await…?

Then, when night falls, curl in and cuddle.

Your mommy will always love you!

Printed in Great Britain
by Amazon